RC

ASPECTS OF BRITISH HISTORY BEYOND 1066

CRIME AND PUNISHMENT

THROUGH THE AGES

Ben Hubbard

raintree
a Capstone company — publishers for children

Raintree is an imprint of Capstone Global Library Limited, a company incorporated in England and Wales having its registered office at 264 Banbury Road, Oxford, OX2 7DY – Registered company number: 6695582

www.raintree.co.uk
myorders@raintree.co.uk

Edited by Helen Cox Cannons
Designed by Philippa Jenkins
Original illustrations © Capstone Global Library Limited 2017
Picture research by Svetlana Zhurkin
Production by Steve Walker
Originated by Capstone Global Library Limited
Printed and bound in China

ISBN 978 1 4747 4135 4
21 20 19 18 17
10 9 8 7 6 5 4 3 2 1

British Library Cataloguing in Publication Data
A full catalogue record for this book is available from the British Library.

Acknowledgements
We would like to thank the following for permission to reproduce photographs: Alamy: Chronicle, 22, Interfoto, 4, Jeff Morgan, 27, Mary Evans Picture Library, 20, 23; Bridgeman Images: Fitzwilliam Museum, University of Cambridge, UK/The Smugglers, 1792 (oil on canvas), Morland, George (1763-1804), 16, Look and Learn/Private Collection/Hunting in the time of William the Conqueror, Jackson, Peter (1922-2003), 8, The Stapleton Collection/Private Collection/Trial by the Ordeal of Boiling Water, illustration from 'Hutchinson's Story of the British Nation', c.1920 (litho), Stewart, Allan (1865-1951), 7; Getty Images: Corbis/In Pictures Ltd., 5, Daniel Allan, 24, Universal History Archive, 21; iStockphoto: duncan1890, 14, 17; Mary Evans Picture Library: cover, 1, 6, 9 (right), Antiquarian Images, 26; Newscom: Ken Welsh, 12, 18, Mirrorpix/NCJ–Topix, 19, World History Archive, 15; North Wind Picture Archives, 10; Shutterstock: Andreas Berheide, cover and throughout (flag), Asmus Koefoed, 30, ayzek, 29, DoodleDance, 28, gualtiero boffi, 9 (left), Tim Saxon, 11, UncleJag, 25

We would like to thank Dr Lesley Robinson for her invaluable help in the preparation of this book.

CONTENTS

Some words in this book appear in bold, **like this**. You can find out what they mean by looking in the glossary.

INTRODUCTION

Can you imagine a time when the punishment for stealing was death by hanging? Or when a person had to dip their arm into boiling water to prove his or her innocence? Would you feel safe owning a cat, knowing that it could have you burned at the stake for witchcraft?

It is hard to believe, but these were all punishments for crimes committed in Britain during the last 1,000 years. Both crime and how the law punishes it has changed a lot during this time. This book explores the story of British crime and punishment over the centuries.

❮ Punishments such as beheadings were common centuries ago.

WHAT IS A CRIME?

A person commits a crime when they break the law. Laws are the rules of society that everyone must obey. Some crimes no longer exist, such as witchcraft. Many people were **accused** of witchcraft simply because they were different from others or did not fit in in their communities. But witchcraft is now no longer against the law, so people are free to claim they are witches if they wish to. Other crimes, such as theft and murder, have always been against the law.

WHY PUNISH?

Over the centuries, there have been different ways of preventing crime and punishing criminals:
A **deterrent** is a punishment so terrible that it stops a person from wanting to commit a crime.
Retribution means a criminal is punished for his or her crime.
Rehabilitation helps a criminal understand that crime is wrong. It also helps the criminal to change his or her ways.

Modern-day prisoners learn new skills as part of their rehabilitation.

A tidy area is a safer area

SAXON AND NORMAN LAWS

In 1066, William the Conqueror came over from Normandy in northern France and invaded England. The country, which had been ruled by the Anglo-Saxons, now belonged to the William and his Normans. To keep control, William kept many Anglo-Saxon laws. These laws included Tithings, Wergilds and Trial by Ordeal.

A WERGILD

A Wergild was a fine paid by a criminal to his or her **victim** or their family. There were different Wergilds for different injuries. Putting out someone's eye cost 50 **shillings**. Cutting someone's ear off cost 6 shillings. The Wergild for killing someone depended on that person's social status.

This illustration shows an Anglo-Saxon man paying a Wergild.

HUE AND CRY

The Hue and Cry meant that if a villager saw a crime, they would cry out (shout). All the villagers were then responsible for catching the criminal. Anyone caught stealing could have a hand, nose or other part of the body cut off. **Treason**, which was a crime against the monarch, was punishable by death.

A TITHING

A Tithing was a group of 10 males over the age of 12 who were responsible for each other. If one of those men committed a crime, the others had to take him to court. If they did not, his punishment was given to every Tithing member.

TRIAL BY ORDEAL

The Anglo-Saxons were a very religious society. They often looked to God to judge crimes. Trial by Ordeal meant asking God to show if a person was guilty. One way of doing this was "ordeal by hot water". The **accused** person had to pick up a stone from a cauldron of boiling water. Their hand was then bandaged and examined three days later. If the wound had healed, God had shown them to be innocent. In reality, that was not long enough for a burn to heal. The accused may well have been innocent.

Ordeal by hot water

NORMAN LAWS

Over time, William the Conqueror introduced his own laws to go alongside those of the Anglo-Saxons. Most were designed to protect the Normans. There was a lot of Anglo-Saxon anger against the Normans. So William introduced something called a Murdrum Fine. This was a one-off sum of money that every person in a region had to pay if a Norman was murdered and the killer not found. This encouraged the villagers to find the killer.

FEARSOME FOREST

William introduced the Forest Law. The law said that in certain woods, no one could cut down trees, carry a bow or hunt the king's deer. Every forest was patrolled, or guarded over, by foresters. The punishment for being caught hunting deer in these areas was having two fingers cut off. Anyone caught more than once was blinded. This was thought to be a powerful **deterrent**.

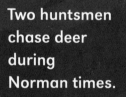

Two huntsmen chase deer during Norman times.

>

Trial by Combat

The Normans introduced the new Trial By Combat. This was a fight between the accused and accuser if nobody else had witnessed, or seen, the crime take place. The fight only finished when one person died or gave up. The loser — if not dead — was then hanged, as God was thought to have judged him to be guilty.

CONFUSING CRIMES

William's system of crime and punishment was extremely unfair. He had all the laws written in French and made it the language of the courts. This meant that Anglo-Saxons accused of a crime could not defend themselves. The accused were often found guilty as a result. William punished murder and other serious crimes with **castration** or blinding.

THE LATE MIDDLE AGES

In 1154, a new king called Henry II took the throne. Henry's barons and **clergy** were rich and powerful. Henry destroyed the castles of barons he did not trust. Then he passed laws to remove power from the Church. First, Henry changed a law named the King's Peace. This was a law that severely punished crimes committed near the king. Henry made this law cover the whole of England.

Henry II made many lasting changes to the English legal system.

HENRY BUILDS JAILS

Next, Henry **abolished** Trial by Ordeal. He said this punishment gave the Church too much power. Instead, Henry set up trial by jury. A jury is a group of ordinary people who decide if someone is guilty or not of a crime. A jury is still used in British law courts today (see page 25). Henry also built jails around the country. These were to hold people while they awaited their court trial.

THE BENEFIT OF THE CLERGY

The Benefit of the Clergy was a 12th-century law. It allowed priests accused of crimes to be tried by the Church courts instead of the king's courts. These laws were not as harsh as the king's courts and never sentenced people to death.

SANCTUARY

If someone was being chased for committing a crime and made it to a church, they could claim **sanctuary**. This meant they had 40 days of protection at the church. They could then face trial or leave the country. Those choosing to leave had to carry a large wooden cross to the nearest port before boarding a ship. The law of sanctuary was abolished in 1623.

A criminal on the run would rap on a sanctuary knocker, such as this one, to be let into the church.

EARLY MODERN BRITAIN

During the 1500s, crime rates rose in Britain. This was partly because the **population** was bigger than before. It was also due to a growing gap between the rich and the poor. Many fell into **poverty** when there was not enough work or food. Some turned to crime to survive. Punishments for begging and stealing were harsh during this period.

A criminal would be in the stocks for several hours or more.

STOCKS AND PILLORY

Fines were a common form of punishment during the 1500s. They were used for minor crimes, such as swearing, drunkenness or gambling. Those who could not pay their fine were placed on public display in a pillory or the stocks. A pillory was a wooden structure that was fastened around a criminal's hands and head. The stocks were fastened around a criminal's ankles. The public would then shame the criminals by throwing rotten food or animal dung at them.

VAGABONDAGE

Vagabonds were unemployed people who moved from town to town looking for work. Some of them also committed crimes, such as begging and **pick-pocketing**. Leaflets about vagabonds frightened local communities, and the law treated them harshly. A vagabond found begging would be whipped and sent away. **Reoffending** vagabonds were sold into slavery, executed or poked through their ear with a red-hot iron.

STURDY BEGGARS

Sturdy Beggars were people who were fit to work but wandered around begging instead. They often came up with cunning ways to steal people's money. A Counterfeit Crank would fake illness on the streets to gain sympathy from passers-by. Those caught stealing anything worth more than one **shilling** were punished with hanging.

HERESY

In 1534, King Henry VIII turned England away from the **Catholic** Church and made England a **Protestant** country. Suddenly it became a crime to practise the Catholic faith. **Heresy**, became the most serious of crimes at this time.

After Henry VIII's reign ended in 1547, England went from being a Protestant country to a Catholic one – and then back again! Therefore people often committed heresy because they just happened to belong to the wrong religion. The punishment for heresy was very harsh. **Heretics** were often burned to death at the stake.

This illustration shows heretics being burned at the stake in 1558.

Terrible treason

Treason was punished with a painful execution. This involved a person being hanged until nearly dead and then being disemboweled, which means having organs removed. The criminal was then beheaded and cut into quarters, which were displayed around the country as a **deterrent**.

THE WITCH TRIALS

In 1542, witchcraft became a crime. During the next 200 years, hundreds of women were **executed** as witches. In 1645, the "Witch Finder General" Matthew Hopkins led a frenzied witch hunt. He accused women of being witches because they had a "witch's mark" such as a mole or wart, or owned a "familiar" such as a cat. To prove their guilt, "ducking" was sometimes used. This involved throwing the accused woman into a pond. If she floated, the pure water was rejecting her and she was a witch. If she sank, she was innocent. However, this also meant that she drowned.

∧ Matthew Hopkins

THREATENING TRADE

In the 1700s vagabondage, heresy and witchcraft were no longer crimes, as the country entered a new era. During this period, some people grew rich and powerful through trade. Crimes that harmed trade were therefore treated very severely. These crimes included smuggling, poaching and highway robbery.

SMUGGLING AND POACHING

Smugglers were people who shipped in goods from abroad without paying taxes on them. These illegal goods were therefore cheaper for people to buy. Many people saw this as a minor "social crime", because they didn't think the goods should be taxed anyway. Poaching, or hunting on someone else's property without permission, was another social crime. Many ordinary people did not think poaching hurt anyone and it helped people to put meat on their tables. Nevertheless the punishments for these crimes could be severe.

Smugglers used ships to > transport stolen goods, such as barrels of tea and alcohol.

HIGHWAY ROBBERY

Highwaymen robbed people travelling on country roads.
Some highwaymen were famous, such as Dick Turpin. They were
seen as "gentlemen robbers" who took from the rich and never hurt
anyone. In reality, many highwaymen were violent murderers.
The punishment for highway robbery was death by hanging.

For rich people, roads were dangerous places to travel along.

THE BLOODY CODE

In 1723, the Waltham Black Act brought in the death
penalty for over 200 crimes. Because many of the listed
crimes, such as poaching and cutting down trees, were
more minor ones, the act became known as the "Bloody
Code". The Bloody Code was designed as a **deterrent** that
would protect the property of wealthy landowners.

INDUSTRIAL BRITAIN

From around 1750, the Industrial Revolution began in Britain. There was also a large rise in the **population** at this time. Many people moved to the towns looking for work in the new factories. This led to overcrowding, disease and **poverty**. As a result, theft and violent crime rose. Under the Bloody Code, many criminals were sentenced to death.

OUT OF CONTROL

Towards the end of the 1700s, public **executions** were getting out of control. Hanging was the most common execution and people were encouraged to go and watch. It was thought hanging would act as a **deterrent**. However, the executions were often treated as entertainment and took on a party atmosphere. At other times, crowds could break out into fights in protest.

Tyburn was London's main setting for public hangings for centuries.

City crime

Criminals found it easy to commit crimes such as **pick-pocketing** in the busy, crowded towns. Some criminals mugged, or attacked, people for their money and possessions. Criminal gangs would jump out on people in dark alleyways and kill them. The streets became a dangerous place to walk.

STREET POLICE

In 1829, during George IV's reign, Home Secretary Robert Peel set up the first professional police force. Policemen became known as "Peelers" and "Bobby's Boys". These policemen patrolled the streets of London dressed in blue uniforms and top hats. They were armed with truncheons (wooden clubs), whistles and handcuffs. These helped to make the streets safer for people to walk on.

A group of Peelers

FINDING OTHER METHODS

During the late 1700s, ideas about punishments began to change. Most people thought that sentencing criminals to death under the Bloody Code was too severe. Because of this, **juries** were less likely to find people guilty. This encouraged criminals because they felt confident a jury would not sentence them to death for their crimes. The government had to find different methods of punishment to execution.

LOCK THEM UP!

An alternative punishment to execution was a jail sentence. Before the 1800s, jails were used to hold an accused person before their court trial. However, after 1800, more people began to be put in jail as punishment.

This illustration shows a crowded cell in Newgate Prison in London. ⟩

PRISON CONDITIONS

Jails were dirty, crowded places where women, men and children were locked up together no matter what their crime. Prison **warders** were not paid and instead earned their money by charging the prisoners. This meant that rich prisoners could afford their own cell, food, beer and even pets! Everyone else had to settle for a corner in a shared cell.

TRANSPORTATION

Instead of receiving the death penalty, criminals could instead face **transportation**. The 1718 Transportation Act meant that a criminal could be shipped overseas, to British **colonies** in the Americas (modern-day USA). Once there, the **convicts** would serve out their sentence working as a labourer or servant for a **colonist**. At the end of their sentence, the convict could return to England. However, many chose to stay and start a new life abroad.

In 1823, Home Secretary Robert Peel **abolished** the Bloody Code. From 1861, the only crimes punishable by death became murder, **treason**, **piracy** with violence and arson in the Royal Dockyards. Arson means setting things on fire on purpose, and the law was to protect the navy's ships in the Royal Dockyards from being set on fire. Transportation was later abolished in 1868. A prison sentence became the main punishment for criminals.

ELIZABETH FRY

In 1813, a **reformer** called Elizabeth Fry (1780–1845) visited London's Newgate Prison. She was shocked at what she found. Hundreds of women were crammed into three small rooms and some of them had babies. There was no bedding and only a bucket to use as a toilet. The women were treated badly by the male prison warders.

> ∧ Elizabeth Fry (centre) was the first woman to campaign for better conditions for female prisoners. She was very brave to go in there.

BUILDING PRISONS

Between 1842 and 1877, 90 new prisons were built in Britain. Prisons for children, called Borstals, were also built. People wanted prisons to **rehabilitate** criminals so they wouldn't **reoffend**. To achieve this, they introduced the "separate system". This kept every prisoner locked up individually. This drove some prisoners mad and others killed themselves. In its place a "silent system" was set up. This meant prisoners could not talk and had to perform pointless labour, such as turning a handle all day. These systems were later replaced with more modern ideas about how to rehabilitate criminals.

JAIL REFORMS

After Elizabeth Fry reported her findings to Robert Peel, he passed a prison reform through parliament called the 1823 Gaols Act. This separated women from men and employed female warders to look after the women. The act also made it law for warders to be paid a wage.

MODERN BRITAIN

The 1900s saw great changes to crime and punishment. The **population** grew further, and the crime rate increased. Technology introduced new crimes to the world. The invention of the radio, television and internet meant that more crime was recorded than ever before. In the 21st century, there was a rise in terrorism and **hate crime**.

This police officer is checking a driver's licence.

POLICING CRIME

Police have more methods than ever to catch criminals. These include CCTV cameras in public places and radios and mobile phones to talk to each other. Computers in squad cars give the police instant access to criminal databases. The police also have powers to look at people's online social media accounts, such as Facebook and Twitter.

MODERN CRIMES

In 1900, cars were a new invention, but during the 1920s they became common. So did car crime. This included minor crimes, such as speeding and parking tickets, but car theft also increased. Computer crime, such as online fraud, grew during the late 1900s. Online fraud is when people trick online computer users into handing over important details, passwords or money.

PUNISHMENT TODAY

In 1964, Peter Allen and Gwynne Evans became the last people to be given the death penalty in Britain. They were hanged for the murder of a man named John West. From that point on, the death penalty was replaced by life imprisonment. This was now the most severe criminal punishment. Jail, fines and community service are the most common punishments for criminals today. Serious crimes are tried in court in front of a jury of 12 people. This is a similar jury system to that introduced by Henry II in the 1100s (see page 11).

CHANGES IN TYPES OF CRIME

Many crimes over the last 1,000 years belong to a particular age. Witchcraft, **vagabondage** and **heresy** were crimes of the Middle Ages. Online fraud and car crime are crimes of the modern era. Other crimes such as theft are as common today as they were in 1066. However, our ideas about punishing crime have changed greatly.

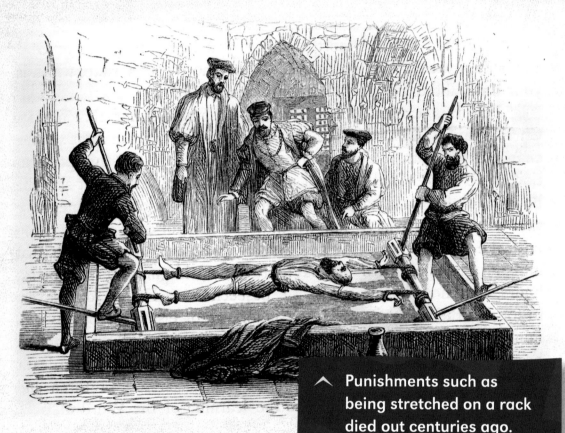

↑ Punishments such as being stretched on a rack died out centuries ago.

CHANGES IN PUNISHMENTS

A criminal caught stealing in the Middle Ages could have a hand, nose, ear or other part of the body cut off. In the 1700s, criminals were given the death penalty or faced **transportation**. Later, during the 1800s, a criminal's loss of freedom was considered to be the ultimate punishment.

Today, physical punishments no longer happen in Britain. For stealing, a criminal now faces a fine, a **community service order** or time in prison. This is because modern punishments are seen as a way of **rehabilitating** criminals. Prisoners are encouraged to work, study and turn over a new leaf.

INTO THE FUTURE

New technologies have added different crimes to those already committed in Britain. These technologies have also made us more aware of crime. In our constantly connected world, crimes are quick to be reported on television news channels and on internet websites. Some court cases are also televised. This can make it feel like crime is on the rise. However, since 1995 the crime rate in Britain has been slowly falling.

Modern-day prisoners are encouraged to read and study. This could improve their lives when they are let out.

TIMELINE

1066
William the Conqueror becomes king. He keeps some Anglo-Saxon laws but adds his own Norman ones.

1154
Henry II extends the King's Peace. This means harsher punishments for crimes across England.

1215
Trial by Ordeal is **abolished**

1494
The **Vagabonds** and Beggars Act says vagabonds should be put in the stocks for three days and three nights

1542
Witchcraft becomes a crime

1718
The **Transportation** Act means that many British **convicts** are transported by ship to the Americas

1723
The Waltham Black Act, known as the "Bloody Code" is introduced

1727
The last woman is executed for witchcraft in Britain

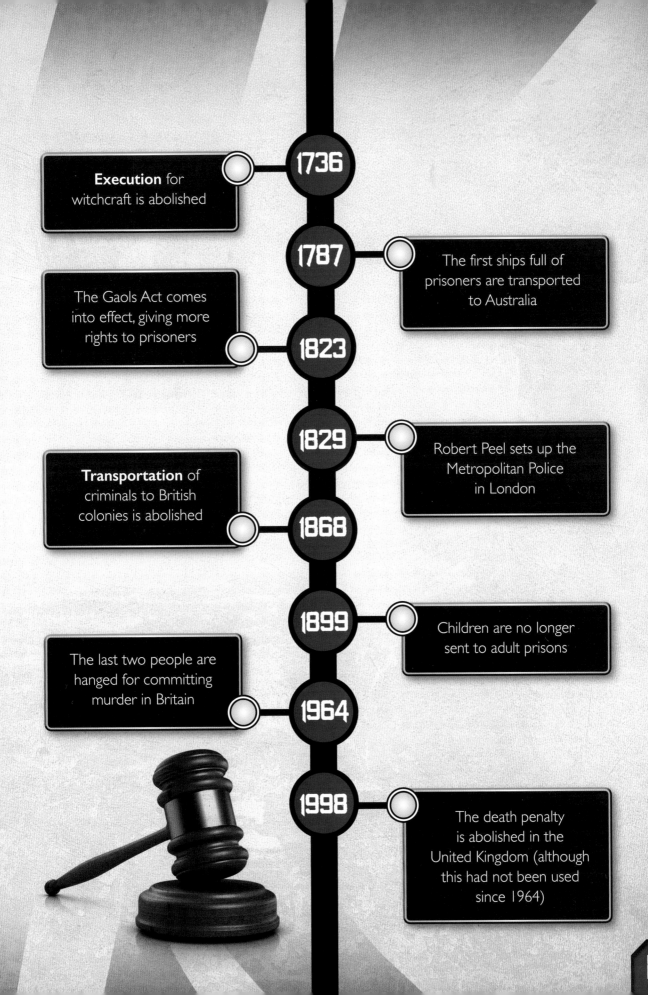

Execution for witchcraft is abolished

1736

1787
The first ships full of prisoners are transported to Australia

The Gaols Act comes into effect, giving more rights to prisoners

1823

1829
Robert Peel sets up the Metropolitan Police in London

Transportation of criminals to British colonies is abolished

1868

1899
Children are no longer sent to adult prisons

The last two people are hanged for committing murder in Britain

1964

1998
The death penalty is abolished in the United Kingdom (although this had not been used since 1964)

GLOSSARY

abolish stop or put an end to

accused person charged with committing a crime

castration removal of a man's testicles

Catholic member of the Roman Catholic church ruled by the Pope in Rome

clergy ministers or priests of the church

colony land in one country that is ruled by another country

community service order punishment given to a criminal instead of jail, such as picking up rubbish within a set area

convict person found guilty of committing a crime

deterrent punishment for a crime that is so bad it stops people from wanting to do it

execution put a person to death as punishment for a crime

hate crime type of crime where a criminal targets a person because of his or her race, colour or gender

heresy having beliefs that do not agree with those of the Church

heretic a person who has been found guilty of heresy

pick-pocketing the stealing of money or valuables from people's pockets

piracy attacking and robbing ships at sea

population number of people living in a country or certain area

poverty having little or no money

Protestant member of the Christian Church which separated from the Roman Catholic Church during the 16th century

reformer person who works to improve society

rehabilitate restore and encourage a prisoner so that they are fit for normal life after they have been in prison

reoffend commit a crime again

retribution punishment for doing something wrong

sanctuary place where someone is protected and given shelter

shilling former British coin equal to 12 pence

transportation the sending of a criminal from one country to a colony

treason disloyal behaviour towards, or crime against, the king or queen

vagabond someone without a home who moves from place to place

victim person harmed, injured or killed as a result of a crime

warder prison guard

FIND OUT MORE

BOOKS

A Photographic View of Crime and Punishment, Alex Woolf (Wayland, 2015)

Banished, Beheaded or Boiled in Oil, Neil Tonge (Wayland, 2016)

Crime and Punishment in Britain, Anne Rooney (Badger Publishing, 2015)

Fighting Crime (Heroic Jobs), Ellen Labrecque, (Raintree, 2013)

WEBSITES

www.bbc.co.uk/education/topics/z6xmn39/resources/1
  This BBC website provides a series of short videos telling stories of real criminals, including children, through the ages.

www.bbc.co.uk/education/clips/zhksr82
  This BBC page about crime and punishment has video clips about the Bloody Code and Trial by Ordeal.

www.nationalarchives.gov.uk/education/resources/victorian-children-in-trouble/
  This website gives information about crime and punishment during Victorian times.

INDEX